LEARN
Tagalog
WORDS

garage
garahe
(gah-RAH-heh)

car
kotse
(KOH-cheh)

friend
kaibigan
(kah-ee-BEE-gahn)

skirt
palda
(PAHL-dah)

dog
aso
(ah-SOH)

BY M. J. YORK • ILLUSTRATED BY KATHLEEN PETELINSEK

Published by The Child's World®
1980 Lookout Drive • Mankato, MN 56003-1705
800-599-READ • www.childsworld.com

Acknowledgments
Translator: Sheila Zamar, Lecturer of Filipino,
University of Wisconsin–Madison

ISBN 9781503835825
LCCN 2019944749

Printed in the United States of America

ABOUT THE AUTHOR

M. J. York is a children's author and
editor living in Minnesota. She loves
learning about different people
and places.

ABOUT THE ILLUSTRATOR

Kathleen Petelinsek loves to draw
and paint. She also loves to travel
to exotic countries where people
speak foreign languages. She lives
in Minnesota with her husband, two
dogs, and a fluffy cat.

CONTENTS

Introduction to Tagalog

Tagalog is a major language of the Philippines. One of its forms, Filipino, is the country's official language. It is used in schools and newspapers. It is spoken by about 40 million people there. It is the fourth-most spoken language in the United States, with 1.6 million speakers in 2015.

Tagalog belongs in the Austronesian language family. It is related to other Philippine languages, including Cebuano. In the past, written Tagalog used the Baybayin alphabet. It grew from Indian writing systems. Today, Tagalog is written using the Latin alphabet. Letters are pronounced as in English with some exceptions.

Tagalog and Filipino are similar but have a few differences. Filipino borrows more words from Spanish and English. This book gives Tagalog words and phrases.

Vowels

a	sounds like **ah** as in f**a**ther
e	sounds like **eh** as in f**ea**ther
i	sounds like **ee** as in s**ee**
o	sounds like **o** as in l**o**ng
u	sounds like **oo** in f**oo**d

Consonants

When **p**, **t**, and **k** begin a word, they are not said with a puff of air as they would be in English.

ng	as in si**ng** can occur at the beginning of a word
q	represents a stop, as in the hyphen in uh-oh
l	like **l** as in se**ll**, not **l** as in **l**eaf
r	like the **r** in red, but flipped as in the Spanish ho**r**a
siy or **sy**	like **sh** as in **sh**ore
diy or **dy**	like **j** as in **j**ust
ts	like **ch** as in **ch**air

My Home
Ang aking tahanan
(Ahng AH-keeng tah-HAH-nahn)

window
bintana
(been-TAH-nahq)

lamp
ilaw
(EE-lahw)

bathroom
banyo
(BAHN-yoh)

bedroom
silid-tulugan
(see-LEED-too-loo-GAHN)

television
telebisyon
(teh-leh-bee-SHOHN)

kitchen
kusina
(koo-SEE-nah)

cat
pusa
(POO-sahq)

living room
sala
(SAH-lah)

sofa
sopa
(soh-PAH)

chair
upuan
(oo-poo-AHN)

table
mesa
(MEH-sah)

6

In the Morning
Sa umaga
(sah oo-MAH-gah)

dresser
tokador
(toh-kah-DOHR)

clock
relo
(reh-LOH)

teddy bear
laruang-oso
(lah-roo-AHNG OH-soh)

doll
manika
(mah-NEE-kah)

pillow
unan
(OO-nahn)

bed
kama
(KAH-mah)

blanket
kumot
(KOO-moht)

comb
suklay
(sook-LAHY)

Good morning! It is seven o'clock.
Magandang umaga!
Alas siyete na.
(Mah-gahn-DAHNG oo-MAH-gah!
ah-LAHS SHEH-teh nah.)

closet
aparador
(ah-pah-rah-DOHR)

brush
panuklay
(pah-nook-LAHY)

shirt
kamiseta
(kah-mee-SEH-tah)

I feel awake.
Gising na gising ako.
(Gee-SEENG nah
gee-SEENG ah-KOH.)

MORE USEFUL WORDS
I feel tired.
Pagod ako.
(Pah-GOHD ah-KOH.)

I feel happy.
Masaya ako.
(mah-sah-YAH ah-KOH.)

dress
bestida
(behs-TEE-dah)

skirt
palda
(PAHL-dah)

pants
pantalon
(pahn-tah-LOHN)

shoes
sapatos
(sah-PAH-tohs)

socks
medyas
(MEH-jahs)

9

At the Park
Sa parke
(Sah PAHR-keh)

sky
langit
(LAH-ngeet)

Let's play!
Maglaro tayo!
(Mahg-lah-ROH TAH-yoh!)

friend
kaibigan
(kah-ee-BEE-gahn) →

soccer ball
bola ng soccer
(BOH-lah nahng SAH-kehr)

bird
ibon
(EE-bohn)

MORE USEFUL WORDS

game
laro
(lah-ROHQ)

sports
isport
(ees-POHRT)

sun
araw
(AH-rahw)

swing
duyan
(DOO-yahn)

cloud
ulap
(OO-lahp)

playground
palaruan
(pah-lah-ROO-ahn)

slide
padulasan
(pah-doo-LAH-sahn)

water
tubig
(TOO-beeg)

pond
batis
(BAH-tees)

flower
bulaklak
(boo-lahk-LAHK)

duck
itik
(EE-teek)

13

airplane
eroplano
(eh-rohp-LAH-noh)

office
opisina
(oh-pee-SEE-nah)

building
gusali
(goo-SAH-leeq)

bus
bus
(boos)

CITY BUS

2100 OFFICE BUILDING

MORE USEFUL WORDS

truck
trak
(trahk)

train
tren
(trehn)

stop
hinto
(heen-TOHQ)

go
abante
(ah-BAHN-teh)

15

My Birthday Party
Ang pagdiriwang ng kaarawan ko

(Ahng pahg-dee-REE-wahng nahng kah-ah-rah-WAHN koh)

I am six years old.
Anim na taong gulang ako.
(AH-neem nah tah-OHNG GOO-lahng ah-KOH.)

grandmother
lola
(LOH-lah)

grandfather
lolo
(LOH-loh)

sister
ate
(AH-teh)

brother
kuya
(KOO-yah)

cake
keyk
(kehyk)

MORE USEFUL WORDS

one **isa** *(ee-SAH)*	eleven **labing-isa** *(lah-BEENG ee-SAH)*
two **dalawa** *(dah-lah-WAH)*	twelve **labindalawa** *(lah-BEEN dah-lah-WAH)*
three **tatlo** *(tat-LOH)*	thirteen **labintatlo** *(lah-BEEN taht-LOH)*
four **apat** *(AH-paht)*	fourteen **labing-apat** *(lah-BEENG AH-paht)*
five **lima** *(LEE-mah)*	fifteen **labinlima** *(lah-BEEN lee-MAH)*
six **anim** *(AH-neem)*	sixteen **labing-anim** *(lah-BEENG AH-neem)*
seven **pito** *(pee-TOH)*	seventeen **labimpito** *(lah-BEEM pee-TOH)*
eight **walo** *(wah-LOH)*	eighteen **labingwalo** *(lah-BEENG wah-LOH)*
nine **siyam** *(SHAHM)*	nineteen **labinsiyam** *(lah-BEEN shahm)*
ten **sampu** *(sahm-POOQ)*	twenty **dalawampu** *(dah-lah-wahm-POOQ)*

18

Time for Dinner
Hapunan na
(Hah-POO-nahn na)

bread
tinapay
(tee-NAH-pahy)

stove
kalan
(kah-LAHN)

pot
kaserola
(kah-seh-ROH-lah)

I am hungry.
Gutom na ako.
(Goo-TOHM nah ah-KOH.)

glass
baso
(BAH-soh)

rice
kanin
(KAH-neen)

meat
karne
(KAHR-neh)

fork
tinidor
(tee-nee-DOHR)

knife
kutsilyo
(koo-CHEEL-yoh)

plate
plato
(PLAH-toh)

spoon
kutsara
(koo-CHA-rahq)

At Night
Sa gabi
(Sah gah-BEE)

MORE USEFUL WORDS

Today is Friday.
Biyernes ngayon.
(Bee-YEHR-nehs ngah-YOHN.)

Yesterday was Thursday.
Huwebes kahapon.
(Hoo-WEH-behs kah-HAH-pohn.)

Tomorrow is Saturday.
Sabado bukas.
(SAH-bah-doh BOO-kahs.)

Good night!
Sige, magandang gabi!
(SEE-geh mah-gahn-DAHNG gah-BEE!)

bathtub
paliguan
(PAH-lee-goo-ahn)

I am tired!
Pagod ako!
(Pa-GOHD ah-KOH!)

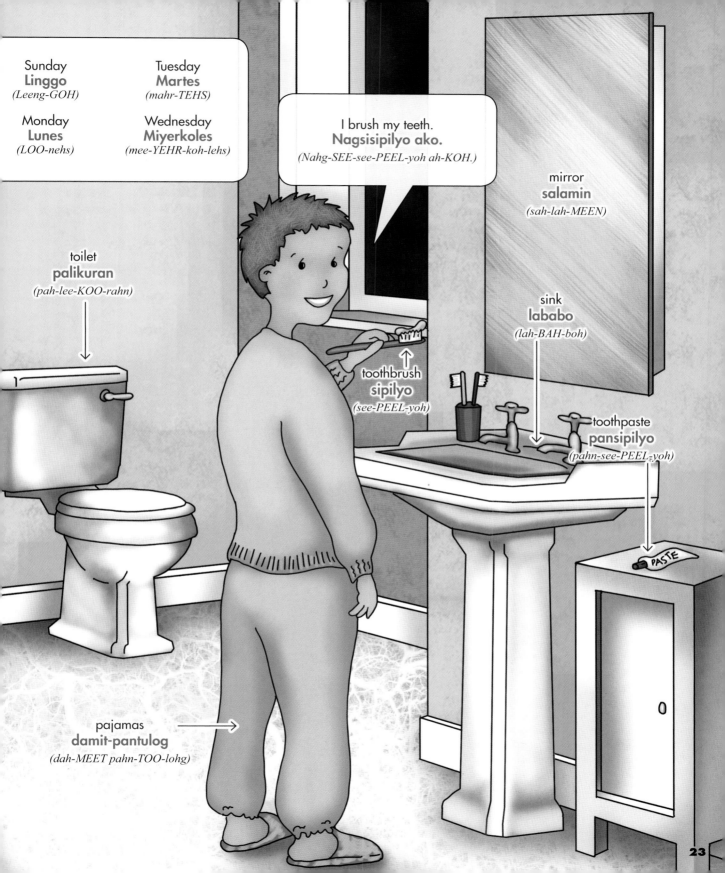

Sunday
Linggo
(Leeng-GOH)

Tuesday
Martes
(mahr-TEHS)

Monday
Lunes
(LOO-nehs)

Wednesday
Miyerkoles
(mee-YEHR-koh-lehs)

I brush my teeth.
Nagsisipilyo ako.
(Nahg-SEE-see-PEEL-yoh ah-KOH.)

mirror
salamin
(sah-lah-MEEN)

toilet
palikuran
(pah-lee-KOO-rahn)

sink
lababo
(lah-BAH-boh)

toothbrush
sipilyo
(see-PEEL-yoh)

toothpaste
pansipilyo
(pahn-see-PEEL-yoh)

PASTE

pajamas
damit-pantulog
(dah-MEET pahn-TOO-lohg)

23

MORE USEFUL WORDS

Yes
oo
(OH-oh)

No
hindi
(heen-DEH)

ten
sampu
(sahm-POOQ)

twenty
dalawampu
(dah-lah-wahm-POOQ)

thirty
tatlumpu
(taht-loom-POOQ)

forty
apatnapu
(ah-paht-nah-POOQ)

fifty
limampu
(lee-mahm-POOQ)

sixty
animnapu
(ah-neem-nah-POOQ)

seventy
pitumpu
(pee-toom-POOQ)

eighty
walumpu
(wah-loom-POOQ)

ninety
siyamnapu
(shahm-nah-POOQ)

one hundred
isang daan
(ee-SAHNG dah-AHN)

January
Enero
(eh-NEH-roh)

February
Pebrero
(pehb-REH-roh)

March
Marso
(MAHR-soh)

April
Abril
(ahb-REEL)

May
Mayo
(MAH-yoh)

June
Hunyo
(HOON-yoh)

July
Hulyo
(HOOL-yoh)

August
Agosto
(ah-GOHS-toh)

September
Setyembre
(seht-YEHM-breh)

October
Oktubre
(ohk-TOOB-reh)

November
Nobyembre
(nohb-YEHM-breh)

December
Disyembre
(dees-YEHM-breh)

winter
taglamig
(tahg-lah-MEEG)

spring
tagsibol
(tahg-see-BOHL)

summer
tag-araw
(tahg-ah-RAHW)

fall
taglagas
(tahg-lah-GAHS)

good-bye!
Paalam!
(pah-AH-lahm!)